MARES MEMORIAL LIB/DICKINSON
DICKINSON PUBLIC LIBRARY

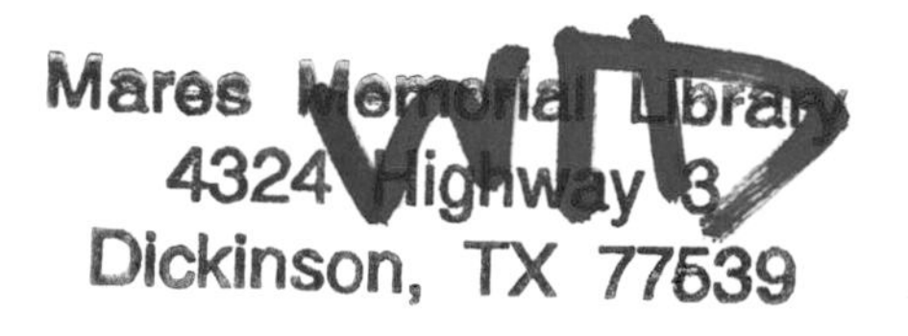
Mares Memorial Library
4324 Highway 3
Dickinson, TX 77539

Henri Matisse

ALBERT KOSTENEVICH

with the collaboration of LORY FRANKEL

HARRY N. ABRAMS, INC., PUBLISHERS

Editor: Robert Morton
Editorial Assistant: Nola Butler
Designers: Liz Trovato with Miko McGinty
Rights and Permissions: Barbara Lyons

Library of Congress Cataloging-in-Publication Data
Kostenevich, A. G. (Al'bert Grigor'evich)
Henri Matisse / Albert Kostenevich ; in collaboration with Lory Frankel.
p. cm.
Includes index.
Summary: Discusses the life of the French painter and makes observations about his work.
ISBN 0–8109–4296–8 (clothbound)
1. Matisse, Henri, 1869–1954—Juvenile literature. 2. Artists—France—Biography—Juvenile literature. [1. Matisse, Henri, 1869–1954. 2. Artists. 3. Painting, French. 4. Art appreciation.]
I. Frankel, Lory. II. Title.
N6853.M33K67 1998
709'.2—dc20
[B] 96–34076

Published in 1997 by Harry N. Abrams, Incorporated, New York

Printed and bound in Hong Kong

Harry N. Abrams, Inc.
100 Fifth Avenue
New York, N.Y. 10011
www.abramsbooks.com

p. 1: Detail of *Blue Tablecloth*. 1909; p. 3: *Two Dancers* (study for *Rouge et Noir*). 1938

CONTENTS

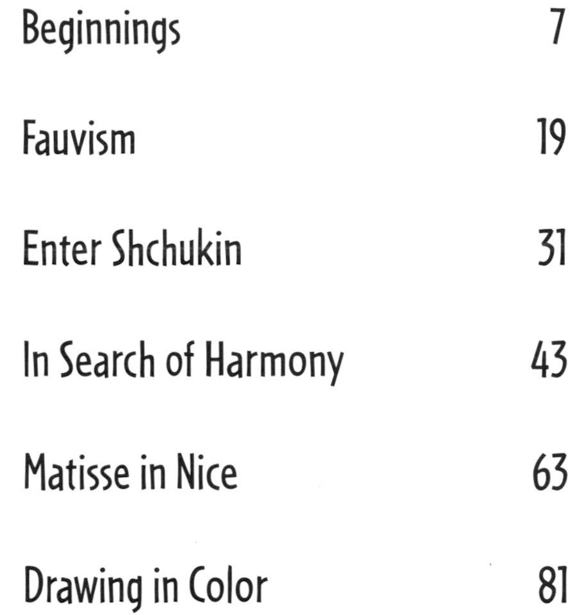

The Cowboy. One of the cut paper illustrations from the book, *Jazz*. 1947

Beginnings

In 1912, when Henri Matisse was forty-two years old, American journalist Clara T. MacChesney visited him in his house and studio in a suburb of Paris (it was represented in one of his best-known paintings, *The Red Studio*). She later wrote, "M. Matisse himself was a great surprise, for I found not a long-haired, slovenly dressed, eccentric man, as I had imagined, but a fresh, healthy, robust blond gentleman, who looked even more German than French, and whose simple and unaffected cordiality put me directly at my ease. Two dogs lay at our feet, and, as I recall that hour, my main recollection is of a glare of light, stifling heat, principally caused by the immense glass windows, open doors, showing glimpses of flowers beyond, as brilliant and bright-hued as the walls within. . . ."

Many other people commented on Matisse's "slow, deliberate speech" and his "serious and reflective air." Some thought he "looked like a German professor with those horn-rimmed glasses he liked to wear." Others found that "his face recalls that of a scientist rather than an artist." Even when he was in art school, his fellow students nicknamed him "the doctor."

The poet Guillaume Apollinaire found Matisse's mild appearance deceptive. He described him as "bearded, with eyes full of mischief behind his gold-rimmed glasses." Painter George L. K. Morris, in a chance encounter with Matisse on a train, began a conversation about art and was rewarded with the emphatic comment that "all artists should have their tongues cut out – then they'd have more time for work." Matisse then illustrated his sentiment by sticking out "a very pink tongue over his beard" and making the gesture of snipping it off with his fingers.

Detail of *The Luxembourg Gardens*. c. 1901–02

Matisse once confided to a friend that among the careers he thought he might have liked were jockey, virtuoso violinist, and actor. Perhaps his strongest characteristic, not apparent to the eye, was his capacity to take risks, to drive himself to the limit. One of his mottoes was "tout ou rien" – all or nothing.

Henri Matisse was born on New Year's Eve in 1869. Then, as now, this was a joyful holiday that held the promise of new beginnings and the hope of new things to come. As an artist, Matisse fulfilled these expectations. Many people consider him the greatest innovator of twentieth-century art as well as a joyful genius who created a world of great beauty and pleasure. Such a gift was not easy in a period that suffered two terrible wars, and Matisse needed a certain strength of mind to set his "art of purity and balance" against the difficulties of life and the horrors of war.

The people of Cambrai, the region where Matisse was born, were famous for strength of mind and persistence as far back as Roman times. Julius Caesar noted the courage and independence of the Nervians, the Gallic tribe that used to inhabit the site where the small town of Le Cateau, Matisse's birthplace, was built. His mother's family, one of the oldest in Le Cateau, was involved in tannery and glove-making from the sixteenth century.

His father moved the family to the nearby town of Bohain, where he sold grain and hardware and kept a pharmacy. As a well-off merchant, he wanted to give his son Henri a good education, with all the trimmings, including violin lessons – although, being practical, he arranged to share the cost by having the teacher give lessons to a neighbor's son as well. But neither Henri nor his friend liked these lessons. When Henri saw the teacher coming, he slipped away and climbed over the fence to his friend's house. By the time the teacher came next door to look for the boys, they had gone back over the fence to hide in Matisse's garden. (At the age of forty-four, Matisse had a change of heart and started to take violin lessons.)

Matisse's father also had his own ideas for his son's career. He sent him to high school for an education in classics and then to Paris to study law. After passing his examination (with an honorable mention), Matisse returned to Bohain and worked as a clerk in a lawyer's office. Although he spent his time doing boring, mechanical work, copying thick piles of files that nobody was eager to consult, he did nothing to change his life.

Self-Portrait. 1900

Not until he was twenty, recovering from an attack of acute appendicitis, did he find his direction. A friend of the family encouraged Henri to take up his own hobby of copying chromolithographs (highly colored reproductions). Although his serious father disapproved of the hobby as a waste of time, his mother, who had a feeling for art, bought him a set of paints, two canvases, and two chromos to copy – a view of a watermill with a riverbank and the entrance to a farm.

Matisse later said, "The moment I had this box of colors in my hands, I had the feeling that my life was there. Like an animal that rushes to what he loves, I plunged straight into it, to the understandable despair of my father.... Before, nothing interested me, after that, I had nothing on my mind but painting."

Matisse painted both copies and signed them Essitam (Matisse backwards). He went on to paint his own pictures, two still lifes. The first, *Still Life with Books and Candle*, shows the remarkable talent of the beginning painter. He created a balanced composition and gave each of the objects a convincing life of its own – in the shine of the copper candlestick, the dullness of the waxen drops, the worn leather of the book covers (law books).

Now Matisse knew he wanted to paint more than anything else – but he

Matisse at the age of nineteen with his mother. 1889
Physically, Henri closely resembled his mother, while displaying the strength of character of his father.

Old Man. 1891
All French art schools required their students to take drawing. Matisse made many pencil and charcoal studies of models from life.

had to get around his father's opposition. For a year he took drawing lessons at six-thirty every morning before going to the office and at six in the evening after he finished work. His teacher gave him encouragement and a letter of introduction to the superstar of French academic painting, Adolphe-William Bouguereau. His mother interceded for Henri when he finally worked up enough courage to ask his father to send him to Paris to study painting. With the promise of a small monthly allowance – but only for a year – he set off for his new life.

Bouguereau did not give Matisse much encouragement. He told the aspiring student that he "didn't know perspective," and Matisse did not thrive in his class. When Matisse failed to get into the Ecole des Beaux-Arts, France's leading art school, he despaired of getting another year's allowance from his father and started saving what he could to get by without it.

Luckily, he found a better teacher. Learning that he might attract the attention of a professor by copying plaster casts in the school's courtyard, he placed himself there and went to work. Gustave Moreau came upon him and invited him to join his studio. So instead of the rule-bound Bouguereau, Matisse had a teacher who was not concerned with rules or academic approval and who let him develop his own style.

Pont Saint-Michel. c. 1900
This is the view Matisse saw every day from the window of his small studio on the Quai Saint-Michel, overlooking the Seine. He made a number of paintings with this subject.

For three years Matisse studied painting with Moreau and took classes in geometry, perspective, and composition. He finally passed the entrance examination for the Ecole de Beaux-Arts, although half of those who also passed got better marks. Still, it was sufficient to maintain his father's support. Earlier, his father had come to visit him in Paris and gave him a real scare. The young Matisse broke out in a cold sweat after waking early one morning to see his half-dressed father standing in front of his studies and drawings, which he had lined up in front of him, as if trying to judge their worth. He also interviewed Moreau, who assured him of his son's talent. But when his father asked his son's chances for the Prix de Rome, a highly sought-after award, and Moreau answered, "Your son is too smart to try for the Prix de Rome," the merchant from Bohain suspected that the professor was mocking him.

However, Matisse was soon able to reassure his father with a different kind of success. His painting *Woman Reading*, of 1895, was bought for the residence of the president of France after being exhibited with four other works in the prestigious Salon de la Société Nationale des Beaux-Arts. This kind of success was what most students of the Ecole des Beaux-Arts dreamed of, and Matisse presented the kind of painting to win such approval: a realistic rendition of an interior showing a delicate interplay of light and shadow. Interestingly, Matisse placed a self-portrait on the wall (above the cupboard), which suggests a silent dialogue between the artist and his model. The woman is Caroline Joblaud, his companion and the mother of his daughter, Marguerite, born a year before.

Matisse was also nominated an associate member of the Société Nationale by Pierre Puvis de Chavannes, its president and one of Europe's most esteemed painters of the time. Only six years after the box of colors set him on the hard road toward a career in painting, the twenty-six-year-old artist saw open to him the road leading to public acclaim, financial success, honors and awards. He did not follow it. He went to Belle-Ile, in Brittany, that summer and met an Australian painter named John Russell, a friend of the Impressionist painter Claude Monet and Vincent van Gogh. He gave or sold Matisse a drawing by the great Dutch artist and he opened to Matisse new horizons. This, to Matisse, was the road worth following. Instead of subdued interiors he painted light-filled seascapes.

His new way of looking permeated *The Dinner Table*, a large and complicated painting intended to display the abilities he had developed after studying at the Beaux-Arts. The leaders of the school found it disappointing. They preferred

Woman Reading. 1895
From the beginning of his career, Matisse painted pictures that combined various genres – here, the still life, the portrait, and the interior – while refusing to bow to popular taste by turning them into stories. He also painted everything from life rather than inventing elements.

heroic subjects – historical or sacred events – and here Matisse gave them plates, cutlery, decanters. Worse, he painted in a style clearly influenced by the hated Impressionism. Moreau, who had no love for Impressionism himself, nonetheless defended the painting. "The decanters," he said, "are so solidly on the table that I could hang my hat on their stoppers."

Moreau managed to bypass the issue of style, teaching his students what was important for any artist: line and color. He urged his students not to be content with copying masterpieces in museums but to go into the street, to learn how to capture quickly the essence of a passerby in a few lines. He also gave his students exercises in which color became all-important. He told them to paint as quickly as possible and without a preliminary drawing in order to keep the color fresh. "If you have no imagination," said Moreau, "you will never do beautiful color.... The color must be thought, dreamed, imagined."

Later that year, Matisse came under the wing of another mentor, the Impressionist Camille Pissarro, who also had advice for the young painter. "Don't proceed by rules and principles, but paint what you observe and feel. Paint generously and unhesitatingly, for it is best not to lose the first impression. Don't be timid in front of nature: one must be bold, at the risk of being deceived and making mistakes. One must have only one master – nature; she is the one always to be consulted." Nature, for both Pissarro and Matisse, did not mean the things they saw around them but the direct and intense feeling of what they saw.

The road Matisse continued to travel took him further and further away from the possibility of academic success – and financial security. At the same time, he met and married Amelie Parayre, and they had two sons in the next two years. Amelie opened a milliner's shop to support the family, but sometimes they had so little money they had to take their children to stay with relatives. When it came to art, Matisse kept his strength of mind and persistence. He had, for example, bought a painting by Paul Cézanne that, he later said, "sustained me morally in the critical moments of my venture as an artist; I have drawn from it my faith and my perseverance." He refused to sell it even when he was desperate for money, because the painting meant more to him – just as his own painting meant everything to him. He wanted to discover – or uncover within himself – a new pictorial language, and he knew it meant a lifetime of working, of searching, of experimenting.

Later in his life, after his efforts brought him financial security on his own terms, Matisse told journalist Clara MacChesney, "Oh, do tell the American people that I am a normal man; that I am a devoted husband and father, that I have three fine children, that I go to the theatre, ride horseback, have a comfortable home, a fine garden that I love, flowers, etc., just like any man." On the outside, Matisse looked like an average middle-class man, but on the inside, he was far from average. He was consumed by art and drove himself hard to achieve his end – which, he could only explain, was what felt right. He did not know it until he had achieved it – and then he had to start looking all over again.

In his search for "what felt right," Matisse traveled to different places. He and his wife went to London so he could study the work of the English painter Joseph Mallord William Turner, who filled his paintings with vivid colors and vibrant light. A month later, they set off for Corsica, where they stayed for six months. The bright sun of the Mediterranean awakened in Matisse a desire to fill his canvases with pure, bright colors. When he returned, he painted several still lifes, using fruits of various colors, red, green, yellow. His room was cold, and he put firewood into the stove but would not clean it, fearing that the ashes would cover the fruit with dust, dimming their color.

Before moving on toward ever brighter color, however, Matisse felt he had to pull back and realize what he had learned. As a result, his next paintings are somewhat darker. Matisse explained what he was after in the painting *The Luxembourg Gardens*, where the trees are depicted as large areas of color, defined only by their outlines. "To paint an autumn landscape," he said, "I will not try to remember what colors suit this season, I will be inspired only by the sensation that the season arouses in me: the icy purity of the sour blue sky will express the season just as well as the nuances of the foliage. My sensation itself may vary, the autumn may be soft and warm like a continuation of summer, or quite cool with a cold sky and lemon-yellow trees that give a chilly impression and already announce winter."

To paint this picture, Matisse got up early and walked to the still empty park, finding the long, cool shadows of the newly risen sun stretched across the path. Here and there, however, the sunlight penetrates the vegetation, and the colors suddenly burn with a vivid flame – as if announcing a new way of painting, extremely simple and vivid.

The Luxembourg Gardens. c. 1901–02
In depicting this popular park, Matisse ignored the orderly garden paths decorated with beautiful sculptures and crowded with strollers. Instead, following Gauguin's example, he treated the scene decoratively, creating a lavishly colorful landscape.

Fauvism

Almost every innovative artist of the twentieth century has created art works that shocked the public and drew scorn and abuse from the art establishment. Matisse's turn came in 1905, when he exhibited ten paintings at the Salon d'Automne. At the center of the storm was *Woman with a Hat*, a portrait of his wife. This was a portrait like none ever seen before. Although his sitter can be recognized, she has an emerald green nose, orange neck, reddish brown hair, and yellow cheeks, the overwhelmingly intense and seemingly absurd colors almost smeared on the canvas, with an evident pleasure but no regard for the usual concerns of the portrait painter.

Art critic Louis Vauxcelles, noting works in a Renaissance style in the center of the room filled with paintings of intense, wild color by Matisse and his friends André Derain, Maurice de Vlaminck, and Albert Marquet, exclaimed, "Donatello among the beasts!" The word for "beasts" in French is "fauves," and Fauvism became the name for the new movement headed by Matisse.

Vauxcelles was one of the few among those who came to see the scandalous pictures to understand what Matisse was trying to do. He said, "Matisse has courage, because his entry – and he knows it – will suffer the same fate as a Christian virgin delivered to the wild beasts in the arena. Monsieur Matisse is one of the most robustly gifted of today's painters. He could have obtained easy bravos: he prefers to drive himself to undertake passionate experiments."

The experiments that led to Fauvism began the summer before, which Matisse spent in Saint-Tropez, a small Mediterranean port. He had been invited by Paul Signac, a leader of the Neo-Impressionists, who had helped to develop an elaborate theory of painting that involved covering the canvas with thousands of separate mosaiclike dots of pure color, rigorously designed to merge optically. For example, green was created not by mixing pigments but by placing dots of blue

A detail of *Bathers With a Turtle*. 1908

and yellow so closely together that the area looked green to the viewer. The Neo-Impressionists' interest in color attracted Matisse, but he found their technique somewhat mechanical, leading to what he felt was a dryness or lack of feeling in the work. However, following Signac, he experimented with the technique in *Luxe, calme et volupté*, "a picture made of pure rainbow colors," as Matisse described it. It was his first composition peopled by imaginary figures and treating the theme of the earthly paradise. Signac, pleased with the work, bought it for his villa in Saint-Tropez.

The following summer, working in a fishing village named Collioure near the Spanish border, Matisse modified the Neo-Impressionist style by using large areas of pure color as well as brief strokes, and he rejected the idea of mixing colors optically rather than on the palette. In paintings such as *View of Collioure*, he created an impression of glistening roof tiles and choppy waves in a sun-filled landscape that knew no shadows.

Moreau, who told his students to use the simplest of means in order to express their feelings most distinctly, predicted that Matisse would succeed in simplifying painting. In the Collioure canvases, Matisse found a way to express his feelings clearly and strongly. These paintings explode with the rebellious energy of the new century.

Matisse was not alone in his desire to free colors from the shackles of convention, allowing them to burst forth in full brightness and vigor. Many younger artists, including Derain, Vlaminck, Marquet, Raoul Dufy, Henri Manguin, and Michel Puy, worked with him toward the same goal. All were labeled Fauvists, although the way each used color differed according to the artist's personality. For example, Derain's work looks simpler and more classical in comparison with the somber and romantic paintings of his close friend Vlaminck.

Matisse and Derain worked in Collioure together in 1905, developing the Fauvist method. As Matisse recalled, "The methods of painting employed by our elders were not adequate to the true representation of our sensations, so we had

Woman with a Hat. 1905

A strikingly bright likeness of Matisse's wife, this portrait triggered a sensation when it was exhibited in the notoriously scandalous Salon d'Automne of 1905 – the show that gave rise to the label Fauvism (the art of wild beasts). The painting reminds us that Matisse's wife opened a small millinery shop to support the family when no one was buying her husband's paintings.

Luxe, calme et volupté. 1904–05
The title comes from a line in Charles Baudelaire's poem "L'Invitation au Voyage" that can be translated as "Luxury, peace, pleasure." It is the first painting Matisse made not from life but from the imagination, although the background shows the Mediterranean coast near Saint-Tropez, where Matisse spent the summer of 1904.

to seek new methods." He told his biographer Gaston Diehl, "We were like children before nature, letting our own natures express themselves freely, with no thoughts of painting without a model when we were not making use of nature itself. I rejected everything on principle and followed my feelings, totally by means of color."

It took a great deal of courage to explore this unknown territory. Derain once said to Matisse, "You paint as if your life depended on it." In any case, the violent attacks his paintings inspired did not discourage him. On the contrary, he carried the new style even further in a large painting called *Le bonheur de vivre (Joy of Life)*, which took five months of concentrated work to complete. It was the only painting he sent to the next major exhibition, the Salon des Indépendants of 1906. Not surprisingly, it also inspired a commotion. Signac wrote to a friend, "Matisse, whose attempts I have liked up to now, seems to me to have gone to the dogs. Upon a canvas of two and half meters [over eight feet] he has surrounded some strange characters with a line as thick as your thumb. Then he has covered the whole thing with flat, well-defined tints, which, however pure, seem disgusting."

In *Joy of Life*, Matisse placed nude figures in a landscape reminiscent of Collioure. The scene of figures dancing, playing music, and making love in a pastoral setting was taken from a Renaissance theme, called the Golden Age, still popular in the nineteenth century. It marked the beginning of a mythological cycle in Matisse's work. Before this, he painted mostly subjects from life – still lifes, portraits, interiors, or landscapes. Now he used ideas in this painting as the point of departure for many important works to follow.

The reclining woman in the center became *Blue Nude* (*Souvenir de Biskra*). The circle of dancers in the background served as the subject for several monumental works on the dance. The group on the left formed the basis for *Le luxe*, a large composition with three nudes. And the crouching woman at the lower left reappears in *Bathers with a Turtle.*

Matisse's composition of *Bathers with a Turtle* evokes the theme of the Three Graces – although his enormous nudes look more like Amazons. Asked once whether he really saw the women as he represented them in such pictures, Matisse answered, "If I met such women in the street, I should run away in terror. Above all, I do not create a woman, I make a picture."

These three giantesses do not belong to our everyday life. They evoke a mythical time. The light emerald green alludes to the unspoiled earth, the dark blue the dreamlike color of the sea. The turtle, which lives on land and in the water, unites

Blue Nude (Souvenir de Biskra). 1907
In May 1906, Matisse traveled to Algeria. From Biskra, he brought back ceramics and textiles that inspired his choice of colors in this painting, which relates to a sculpture he made at the same time. Both works reflect a heightened sensuality that the artist experienced in the heat and brilliant sunlight of north Africa.

Joy of Life (Le bonheur de vivre). 1905–6
This large, imaginary composition is central to the period when Matisse was developing Fauvism. The leading art critics accused Matisse of intentionally ignoring the eternal principles of art. Matisse's interest here, however, was in creating a new kind of harmony. The painting parallels the world described in Stéphane Mallarmé's poem "L'Après-midi d'un faune": "These nymphs, I want to keep them alive./ So clear,/ Their light rosiness, which fills the air/ Drowsy with luxuriant slumbers."

the figures and the background, serving as a symbol for the beginning of the world.

Matisse once gave an interview to a Russian journalist named Belevsky, who questioned the painter closely about this work. He started by asking Matisse to explain why he had painted it in this way.

Matisse looked at the picture and said, low and thoughtfully, "Look. In this picture I wanted to achieve a curved line that I like. It mounts upward and continues with a slight bend, then, after it is broken off, it moves down here. Do you see it? It was this line that I wanted to do. The grouping gives it. I put two figures here, and there – one. There both is and isn't a symmetry. In any case, the general outline is full of harmony."

The journalist replied, "Very well. To create this harmony you gave the women triangular heads. But why have you made the leg of one bather weak and of another athletic and ended it with a walrus flipper?"

"But why must I draw the legs with all the details? Do you think I cannot draw the leg anatomically correct?" Matisse grabbed a pencil and a piece of paper and began to draw a leg very quickly. In a minute he had sketched the entire leg perfectly – hip, kneecaps, calf, ligaments.

"You see? And now what? Do you demand small veins, hairs, and pores? But I am not a photographer. I am an artist, and I have no need for all that. What do I need? I need the basic lines of the body given in correct proportion and placed correctly and logically. You call this leg weak. But look. The measurements between the head of the femur and the knee, then between the knee and the instep are relatively correct. The angle of the leg is right relative to the position of the body. All the weight of the body is on the foot that leans heavily on the ground; that is why it is represented so big. So, this leg actually has everything necessary. And I'm not interested in the calf and hairs."

"What about the flipper?"

"But it completes the curve of the back. Do you see that this way the line ends agreeably?" Matisse drew a curve in the air with his finger, as if enjoying the trajectory, which left no trace. "In sum," he continued, "I don't paint unnecessary and illogical things. You criticized me earlier for giving my dancers [in *Dance II*] not hands but something shapeless. But think about it. They are dancing and moving quickly in a circle. Can we see the hands of people moving fast? What can we see? Certainly not fingernails, and you would not make me draw them. You would, I imagine, excuse the fingers, too. What is left? Just what is in the picture."

Most of the public – and most critics and other artists, as well – had similar dubious reactions to Matisse's art. Critic Roland Dorgelés, only half joking, wrote, "Matisse has done more harm in a year than an epidemic! Matisse causes insanity!" Charles Morice, an artist sympathetic to but puzzled by Matisse's work, commented in 1908 that Matisse "continues to worry his enemies without reassuring his friends."

Fortunately for Matisse, there were a few collectors bold enough to buy his work. The Stein family from San Francisco – Gertrude and her brother Leo –

Bathers with a Turtle. 1908

Matisse owned Paul Cézanne's painting *Three Bathers*, which he considered his talisman. He made a version of three bathers that was simpler and more monumental than Cézanne's, treating his figures symbolically, as embodiments of the eternal power of nature. He included a turtle probably because he knew that in some cultures the turtle is seen as a sacred animal, an embodiment of a life force.

bought *The Woman with Hat* (it later came down to Michael Stein and his wife Sarah, who was a student of Matisse). While their interest did not last very long, they introduced Matisse to another collector, Etta Cone, and others soon appeared. The German Karl-Ernst Osthaus bought *Bathers with a Turtle*, and the Russian Sergei Shchukin, regretting that he had missed his chance to buy the latter, acquired *Game of Bowls*.

A counterpart to *Bathers with a Turtle*, *Game of Bowls* shows three nude figures, here boys, in a very similar setting. It, too, derives from the theme of the Golden Age, although it lacks the idyllic quality usually associated with the genre. The youths are thoroughly absorbed in their game, not, as one might think, *pétanque*, a bowling game very popular in the south of France, but, as indicated by the almost ritualistic poses and gestures, the "game of life." The extremely simplified background becomes the only appropriate setting for the serious and mysterious symbolic action. The boys, nude to express humanity's primal state, are three in number, like the Fates, and they play their game of chance and skill with three balls. As in the earlier picture, the blue symbolizes the sea or river, itself a symbol of the unity of life and death, while the green of a meadow represents not only life but also the color of Osiris, the Egyptian god of nature's productive life and lord of the afterlife.

This painting and others of the same period show the first visible signs of Matisse's interest in the art of non-European cultures. For many years, he had explored many different cultures. In 1903, he visited an exhibition of Islamic art; in 1905 a show of French primitive painters of the later Middle Ages. In 1907, he remarked to Guillaume Apollinaire that an artist seeking to develop an individual style can learn much from studying many varieties of artistic expression, whether of the ancient Egyptians, Greeks, Cambodians, Peruvians, or Africans. In his own search for the very roots of all art, for its spiritual elements, Matisse found himself attracted to the magic of primitive ritual, the meditativeness of the East, and medieval Christian spirituality. Both exotic art and children's drawings helped him to unlock the primordial mystery of art.

Game of Bowls. 1908

In this counterpart to *Bathers with a Turtle*, Matisse used male figures instead of female bathers and the same simplified background to create another symbolic composition. Sergei Shchukin, the Russian collector, saw the painting in Matisse's studio soon after he had begun it and asked the artist to finish it for him.

Enter Shchukin

Sergei Shchukin was the third son of a wealthy Russian merchant, a small, sickly child with a stutter so bad he was tutored at home instead of going to school. To everyone's amazement, he became one of the richest and most powerful businessmen in Russia. Greatly influenced by the relative solitude in which he spent his early years and the constant effort to overcome his stuttering, he grew up to be a bold, decisive man. He never mastered his speech defect, but he prepared to take on the world.

Like the textile business, collecting art ran in the family: three of his five brothers were leading art collectors, each with his own specialty. Sergei began what would become a fabled collection with landscapes by the Impressionist painter Claude Monet. The boldness of his choice at the time is indicated by the fact that a visitor to his house wrote some indignant words right on one of Monet's canvases.

From Monet, Shchukin moved on to Paul Gauguin, Vincent van Gogh, and Paul Cézanne. The artist Leonid Pasternak, father of the poet and novelist Boris, recalled, "Once I was at Shchukin's place. 'I'll show you something,' he said. Opening slightly a heavy drapery, he took out his first Gauguin. . . . Laughing and stuttering, Shchukin said, 'A ma-ma-madman painted it and a ma-ma-madman bought it.'"

Shchukin was far-seeing rather than mad, but he knew that most of Moscow society found his taste in art shocking and bizarre and probably judged him by the art he kept. His appearance gave no hint of the passionate collector of radical new art. Matisse described him as "about fifty years old, a vegetarian, extremely sober." Shchukin, however, was committed to establishing for Moscow a gallery containing the most influential and daring new European art of the period. Like Matisse,

Detail of *Harmony in Red*. 1908–09

he saw in modern painting a logical extension of universal principles dating back to the ancients. "In Paris," Matisse later recalled, "Shchukin's favorite pastime was to visit the Egyptian antiquities of the Louvre, where he found parallels with Cézanne's peasants."

Shchukin met Matisse in 1906 and immediately grasped his importance for modern art. That is, almost immediately: Matisse related that Shchukin visited his Paris studio and was attracted to a still life. Before he would buy it, he told Matisse he had to take it home and live with it for several days, "and if I can bear it and remain interested in it, I'll keep it."

Shchukin kept the painting and bought many more. Among them was a large canvas he saw in Matisse's studio, *Harmony in Blue*, which he wanted for his dining room, to go with a group of eighteen Tahitian pictures by Paul Gauguin.

Matisse, while still working on the painting, promised it to the Russian. He was preparing this major work for the Salon d'Automne of 1908 when he felt an irresistible impulse to rework it. He wrote to Shchukin that he had considered the painting finished and hung it on the wall of his studio to study it. "Later I felt it was not decorative enough and could do nothing else but start work on it again, for which I am

Portrait of Sergei Shchukin. 1912
Matisse made this magnificent drawing as a preparatory study for a painting of his patron (below). However, while posing for this portrait Shchukin learned of his brother's death and immediately left Paris to return to Moscow. The painting was never done.

Blue Tablecloth. 1909

Matisse applied full color to all the objects, omitting shadows. The picture combines two different points of view: the objects–chocolate pot, fruit dish, and decanter–seen from the front, and the tablecloth seen from above.

Harmony in Red or *Red Room.* 1908

When Matisse began this painting, he called it *Grande nature morte* – large still life. Destined for Shchukin's main dining room, it repeated the subject of the early *The Dinner Table*, here treated with remarkable simplicity and vigor. The contours of the trees, the fruit on the table, and the woman's figure echo the strong curving pattern of the decorative tablecloth.

delighted today. Even those who thought that it was well done at first now find it considerably more beautiful." *Harmony in Blue* had become *Harmony in Red*.

A visitor to Matisse's studio commented on the revision by saying it was a different picture. Matisse responded, "He does not understand a thing. It's not a different picture. I am seeking forces and a balance of forces." He observed that the red-green-blue-black surface could be overpainted in blue-white-red-green, but it would still be the same picture. The same feeling would be presented, only with different rhythms. "The difference between the two canvases is that of two aspects of a chessboard in the course of a game of chess."

Harmony in Red, or *Red Room*, as it was also called, represents a turning point in European art. In it, Matisse used extremes of color without losing sight of the fact that the goal of art is harmony. This was the first of many monumental painting compositions dominated by a single color, which Matisse likened to musical compositions. He strove to reach his goal, what he once called "the shining independence of color," through these works. Here, color equals the interior as subject and lifts the painting to a different, symbolic realm.

Shchukin accepted the greatly revised painting (Matisse lowered the price somewhat, perhaps as a kind of apology) and thereafter put his complete trust in Matisse, keeping up with his every creative step. Matisse, knowing he could count on Shchukin's support, may have felt freer to push his experiments to the limit. One after another, his boldest pictures made their way to Moscow.

One of these, *Conversation*, was begun soon after *Harmony in Red*, although it took Matisse four years to finish. Another monumental interior with figures, it, too, represents a room looking out onto a brightly lit garden, and it, too, is dominated by a single color, an intense blue.

After Matisse began work on the picture he wrote an essay, "Notes of a Painter," in which he said, "When I see the Giotto frescoes at Padua I do not trouble myself to recognize which scene of the life of Christ I have before me, but I understand the sentiment that emerges from it, for it is in the lines, the composition, the color. The title will only serve to confirm my impression." The previous year, Matisse had visited Italy and was much taken with the work of the pre-Renaissance painter Giotto, whose frescoes contained a magnificent blue.

What is this conversation about between the man in pajamas and the woman in bathrobe early on a summer morning? Matisse admitted that the characters here are himself and his wife. While the painting is a portrait, it is also an interior and, most important, a large decoration in which the characters, their story, and the room serve merely as pretexts for the composition.

The beautiful blue that surrounds the characters can be understood symbolically as their emotional focus, their mental concentration. The color also calls to mind the shadowiness of the room. The Impressionists were the first to find blue in shadows, but Matisse used it in a much more radical way: the blue is not shadow itself but a link between two worlds – the physical, in which every illuminated object has a shadow, and the spiritual, governed by the artist's sense of beauty, the world to which his feelings and imagination belong.

Matisse always tried to emphasize not the objects themselves but the relationships between them. For this reason, he did not want to have his painted objects cast real shadows, which are appropriate only for creating an illusion of real space. He realized that a canvas is not real space but flat, and he wanted his pictures to respect its flatness. Even the gap of window that opens onto the garden does not create an impression of depth, as Matisse reduced the lawn to a simple, flat surface, broken up with patches of blue to relate it to the interior.

The highpoint of the relationship between Henri Matisse, artist, and Sergei Shchukin, collector, was the latter's commission of two large panels for the stairwell of his mansion in Moscow. The proposal allowed Matisse to realize his dream of creating a great decorative ensemble. Matisse conceived an ambitious project: "I imagine a visitor coming in from outside. There is the first floor. One must summon up energy, give a feeling of lightness. My first panel represents the dance, that whirling round on the top of the hill. On the second floor one is now within the house; in its silence I see a scene of music with engrossed participants; finally, the third floor is completely calm and I paint a scene of repose; some people reclining on the grass, chatting or daydreaming. I shall obtain this by the simplest and most reduced means; those which permit the painter pertinently to express all of his interior vision."

Matisse was actually describing his earlier painting *Joy of Life*, divided into three panels. Unfortunately, Shchukin's residence could not accommodate this program: his mansion, an elegant eighteenth-century building, had only two floors, not three, and the staircase was rather small. Matisse chose the dance and the scene of repose and sent sketches to Shchukin in Moscow. The dance composition attracted the collector almost at once (he saw the first version of it, *Dance I*, now at the Museum of Modern Art, New York). However, in a significant exception to his usual behavior, he rejected the scene of repose. He wrote to Matisse, "I

Conversation. 1909–12

In this monumental composition, Matisse superimposed two different levels of meaning. On the face of it, it is a genre scene depicting an early morning conversation between husband and wife. At the same time, it transports us to an entirely different realm, that of the supernatural, its morning stillness evoking the magic of paintings of the Annunciation. At the time that he was working on this painting, Matisse wrote, "What most interests me is neither still life nor landscape but the figure. It is through the figure that I come closest to expressing the nearly religious feeling I have toward life."

find your panel the *Dance* of such nobility that I have resolved to brave our bourgeois opinion and to place upon my staircase a subject with *the nude.* At the same time, I will need a second panel for which the subject might very well be music.... We have a great deal of music in my house. About ten concerts of classical music (Bach, Beethoven, Mozart) are given each winter. The music panel should indicate some of the character of the house."

Matisse complied with a panel on music, but it had nothing to do with classical music concerts in Shchukin's mansion. Both panels, *Dance II* and *Music,* are highly energetic, with nude figures set in a primitive landscape similar to those of *Bathers with a Turtle* and *Game of Bowls.* Before sending them to Shchukin,

Dance I. 1909

Matisse completed this canvas in one or two days – a remarkably short period of time. The subject comes from the ring of dancers in his painting, *Joy of Life.* Matisse removed one figure to adapt it to a large decorative surface and give it balance.

Matisse exhibited them at the 1910 Salon d'Automne, where they did not get a favorable response. Many critics were so nonplussed by them that they refrained from comment altogether. Even Shchukin found they needed getting used to. He wrote, "I am beginning to enjoy looking at your panel the *Dance*, and as for *Music*, that will come in time."

Matisse made two versions of the dance panel and repainted the music panel at least twice. Since both panels were to hang side by side, the artist had to do whatever he could to unify them. His first version of the dance was not dynamic

Dance II. 1910

In a book about art, Matisse wrote, "I love dance. Dance is an extraordinary thing: life and rhythm. I find living with dance easy. When I had to create a composition on dance for Moscow, I simply took myself to the Moulin de la Galette one Sunday afternoon. And I watched the dancing, especially the farandole. . . . When I got home, I composed my dance on a surface of four meters [13 feet], singing the same tune I had heard at the Moulin de la Galette, so that the entire composition, all the dancers, came together and danced to the same rhythm. . . ."

Music. 1910

Matisse loved music. Until the age of fifty, he played the violin; in this painting, he placed the violinist at the left edge of the panel, where he serves as a kind of clef in music notation. In this work, Matisse was looking to create a visual equivalent of music through color. The blue and the green were inspired by the sky and the foliage of the French Riviera, and were combined with the color of the unclothed human body to express an elemental harmony.

enough. The final work embodied a magnificent, tightly sprung power, and the static music panel was conceived as a counterbalance to the dance. But the calm of *Music* was not of the relaxed variety; it was an animated and creative calm, the calm that is a match for motion.

The action of the two panels is obvious: women dance in the first and men sing or play musical instruments in the second. In this respect, the figures personify the two forms of art—not by the simple act of dancing and making music but by giving themselves entirely to the two arts. The theme of the two panels could thus be interpreted as humanity's relationship to life as mediated by art – a subject of tremendous importance to Matisse.

But the action here goes beyond the creative act. The primeval dance was also a manifestation of magic. In very early times, the dance performed by people clasping hands signified the union of earth and sky. The hill or mountain (the rise of earth on which the characters dance) also traditionally symbolized the union of earth and sky and was therefore associated with an ascent to the realm of the spiritual. Music was often used to symbolize universal harmony. The theme is represented also by the male and female characters: Woman *(Dance II)* stands for the principle of union, man *(Music)* for individualism.

A year after he sent these two panels to Moscow, Matisse, at Shchukin's invitation, went to Russia. While he was there, Matisse rearranged Shchukin's collection of his works. He insisted on placing them in the same room and selected for the purpose the drawing room, which was decorated in pink. When the paintings did not fit into the spaces between the molded medallions on the walls, Matisse put them directly over the medallions. The contrast between the sumptuous eighteenth-century room with its pink sofas and porcelain and Matisse's bold, strongly colored art, often described as "barbaric," must have been remarkable.

The aspect of Russia that most impressed Matisse was its icons, religious paintings, usually small and intense. In an interview he gave in Moscow, Matisse exclaimed at their "wealth and purity of color," their "spontaneity of expression." "I am familiar with the religious art of several countries," he said, "and nowhere have I ever seen such a complete expression of the mystic mood, at times even of religious fear."

In Search of Harmony

It was Sergei Shchukin who, after seeing Cézanne's painting *The Card Players*, suggested that Matisse create a "composition with clothed figures. Perhaps a portrait of your family (Madame Matisse and your three children)." Matisse was not about to do a work in the manner of Cézanne. However, he had recently gone to Munich to see an exhibition of Muslim art, which made a strong impression on him, especially the Persian miniatures. For *The Painter's Family*, he used the principles of the Persian miniature, applying them on a monumental scale. This picture and three others form a group of works that were later termed symphonic interiors.

The Greek word *symphonia* means harmony, a pleasing combination of notes sounded together. A symphony orchestra employs a wide range of different instruments, all playing together in the same key to create harmonious music. Matisse was interested in exploring the complex relationship among colors and the different elements of a painting. Ironically, studying the Persian miniature – a very small, bright, and delicate painting – Matisse said, helped him "to break out of the limits of intimate painting." No subject is more intimate than a family scene, yet Matisse turned it into a monumental, complex symphony of color and figure and pattern. The figures – his wife, engaged in needlework in the left background, his two sons, Pierre and Jean, playing checkers, and his daughter, Marguerite, at right – stand out starkly as bold areas of color against the intricately patterned carpet, sofa, wallpaper, and fireplace. The checkerboard serves as an overall motif for the picture's structure, linking together the diverse elements.

While working on this painting, Matisse wrote to his friend and collector Michael Stein, "The picture is going well, but since it is not finished yet, that does not mean anything. It's not logical but I am not sure it will be a success. This all or nothing is very tedious."

Detail of *Landscape Viewed from a Window*. 1912

The Painter's Family. 1911

Matisse, who adored Cézanne, agreed to paint a family portrait for Shchukin. However, he did not want to follow Cézanne's style. The result challenged not only its model but also the art of the period: it stands like a monumental bridge between two different civilizations, marrying traditional Eastern ornament to the modern Western dynamic.

The Red Studio, another of the symphonic interiors and the greatest of Matisse's works on this subject, shows his working space in Issy-les-Moulineaux, a suburb of Paris. Since this is where the artist creates, the room is filled with his personality. Although no one is shown in the studio, we feel a human presence at once. Someone hung these canvases on the wall, placed the sculptures on stool-pedestals, prepared the frame to receive a painting, leaned a picture against the chest of drawers to look at it more closely. That "someone" is the artist, and all of these objects are essential parts of his existence. The focus of this existence is art, the transfiguration of the objects to endow them with a new harmony and beauty.

Paul Cézanne. *The Card Players.* 1890–92
Shchukin had this picture in mind when he suggested that Matisse do a large-scale portrait of the artist's family.

Pink Statuette and a Pitcher on a Red Chest of Drawers. 1910

Matisse treated the space more abstractly than ever before. It is hard to tell where ceiling and wall meet or where the floor begins. The powerful red floods the room, like a sea in which the objects – mostly artworks by the artist – resemble islands. In the center stands a clock with no hands, reminding us that painting aims to fix a moment, not to show the movement of time, and in this way art overcomes time.

Soon after Matisse finished *The Red Studio* in 1911, a visitor came to his studio. "You are looking for the red wall?" asked the artist. "That wall does not exist at all! As you can see here, I painted the furniture against a purely blue-gray studio wall.

The Red Studio. 1911
Matisse thought very highly of this painting, sending it to important exhibitions in London and New York (the famous Armory Show). In it, the real (the objects of the artist's studio) and the imaginary (the overall red and other magical colors) coexist in a natural way. Red was one of Matisse's favorite colors; in his self-portraits, he often portrayed himself wearing red.

These are the sketches, the studies, if you will; as paintings they did not satisfy me. When I found the color red, I put the studies in the corner, and there they remain. . . . Where did I get this color red? My goodness, I don't know."

Matisse began 1912 with his first trip to Morocco. Many years later, Matisse told poet and critic André Verdet, "Morocco had excited all my senses. . . . The intoxicating sun long held me in its spell." In the fall of 1912 he went back for a much longer stay. These two voyages to Morocco renewed his connection with nature and opened up a new path for his art.

He painted what is known as the Moroccan Triptych for Ivan Morosov, another great Russian collector, who already possessed a large group of Matisse's still lifes. This series of the paintings *Landscape Viewed from a Window*, *On the Terrace*, and *The Casbah Gate* formed his next great ensemble after *Dance II* and *Music*. The three works share common dimensions and the dominance of blue in different tones to suggest the deep southern sky, the shadows of trees or walls, a windowsill, or a carpet.

Landscape Viewed from a Window uses a structure similar to *Conversation*, with the human figures replaced by two bouquets of flowers engaged in a wordless dialogue. In *On the Terrace*, the woman (Matisse's favorite Moroccan

Goldfish. 1912
Every element of this picture – lines, circles, ovals; leaves, flowers, table – expresses the slow and mesmerizing circular movements of the fish inside the bowl. The colors, too, focus attention on the bright red fish.

Landscape Viewed from a Window. 1912
Matisse wrote to Morosov that he painted three of his Moroccan pictures to be seen together, *Landscape Viewed from a Window* on the left, *The Casbah Gate* on the right, and *On the Terrace* in the center.

On the Terrace. 1912

The Casbah Gate. 1912
Matisse's archives contain a postcard of the Casbah gate, which he may have used in painting this canvas. Comparing the two, we see that he eliminated all the houses but one and many smaller details, such as the stones of the pavement, in order to let the color take over the composition.

model, named Zorah) seems to swim in the ethereal blue that takes over the walls and floor, whose junction is invisible. *The Casbah Gate,* like *Landscape Viewed from a Window,* gives a far view of the city framed by a tableau of intimacy. The faraway figures in *Landscape,* caught in the blinding sunlight on the square, introduce the human theme, like music first heard at a distance, a function served by the shadow-cloaked figure in *The Casbah Gate.* The theme is fleshed out in the central scene of the triptych, *On the Terrace.* The terrace acts as a transition between interior and exterior, just as the window and gate are transitions between the world within and the world beyond. At the terrace, the entrance to the house, Arabs leave their shoes to enter a realm governed by different rules, or they emerge from the house to sit and take the air, to survey the drowsy neighborhood. Zorah, seated on a rug, seems to float in a magical space where the shoes coexist with golden fish in a bowl.

The goldfish also appear in *Moroccan Café,* the largest and most important picture of the Moroccan period. Matisse did not immediately find his way to its ultimate simplicity and abstraction. The preparatory drawings, hastily sketched from life, captured in a few strokes several concrete details – the pose of a dozing Arab, a man's head thrown back to drink, the Moroccans

Moroccan Café. 1912–13
Marcel Sembat wrote of this painting, "The longer you look at it, this picture of a Moorish café, the more there rises up in you a sense of dreamy contemplation." Shchukin wrote to Matisse from Moscow that he considered this his favorite picture, and he spent not less than an hour in contemplation of it every day.

seated on their small carpets with their shoes set down beside them. Matisse originally used a row of shoes to form the lower border but painted over them in the end. He made many other changes as well. His friend Marcel Sembat, writing about this painting, noted, "consciously or not, deliberately or in spite of himself, every time he has attempted to improve something he had done, he has moved in the direction of simplicity. A psychologist would make no mistake about it; Matisse instinctively moves from the concrete to the abstract and the general. I have told him this. 'The thing is,' he answered me, 'I move the way my feelings point, toward ecstasy. . . . Then, too,' Matisse continued, 'it's how I find peace of mind.'"

In the next several years, as World War I erupted in Europe, peace of mind was hard to come by. Matisse's relatives in Bohain ended up behind enemy lines, and his brother had been taken hostage. Many of his friends joined the army. Matisse, forty-four years old, tried to enlist but was rejected. He went with his friend Albert Marquet to see Marcel Sembat, who had become a cabinet minister. "Derain, Braque, Camoin, Puy are all at the front, risking their skins. . . . We are sick of staying behind. How can we serve our country?" Sembat answered them, "By continuing to paint as well as you do."

During these difficult years, Matisse returned to the subject of Morocco, perhaps hoping to escape from the world of anxiety and tension into the earthly paradise and peace the country symbolized for him. But the real world followed him into his art. *The Moroccans* shows the world of black night, although Matisse implied that the black set off the painting's luminosity. "Doesn't my painting *The Moroccans* use a grand black which is as luminous as the other colors in the painting?"

In the painting, Matisse converted the figures of Arabs on the terrace of a small café into geometric forms. Years later, he described this work as "the beginning of my expression in color, with blacks and their contrasts. They are reclining figures of Moroccans, on the terrace, with their watermelons and gourds."

Black became the dominant color of his paintings during the war. When Matisse met Auguste Renoir for the first time, the aged artist admitted that he did not like the younger man's work. He would even have gone so far as to say that Matisse was a bad painter were it not for the way he used black. While the other Impressionists usually avoided black, the problem it presented attracted Renoir, and in some pictures he made it a key element. Matisse's ability to make it work

The Moroccans. 1915–16
Matisse wanted to start work on this picture soon after he returned from his second trip to Morocco, but he had to postpone it. Although his Moroccan impressions show up in the colors, influenced by Arab decorative art, tiles, and textiles, the spirit reflects instead the difficult years during World War I.

for him in the simplest and most effective way convinced Renoir that Matisse was indeed an artist of note.

These pictures gain drama and strength not only from the color black but also from their striking rectangular forms. In *White and Pink Head,* Matisse used geometric shapes as well as colors to create a portrait. The head is set against a simple black back-ground. Remarkably, the simplification somehow helps to create a likeness of his daughter, Marguerite.

Matisse once said, "For me nature is always present. As in love, all depends on what the artist unconsciously projects on everything he sees. It is the quality of that projection that gives life, in the eyes of an artist, rather than the presence of a living person." For his *Portrait of Greta Prozor,* Matisse started with the actual person sitting for him but was unable to complete the picture. He apologized to Greta and stopped work. Several years later, Greta was astonished to find her portrait at an exhibition. Matisse had managed to find a way to finish the picture without having the model in front of him. His own state of mind, rather than impressions from the model, led the way for him.

In Matisse's portraits, the background may be as expressive as the model. In *Portrait of Auguste Pellerin (II),* Matisse merged the black background and the sitter's coat to give the portrait a look of severity.

Matisse painted the portrait of Auguste Pellerin, a man who had become wealthy selling margarine, at the sitter's request, which was unusual for Matisse. Even more unusual, he agreed to paint a second portrait if Pellerin, an important collector of art, did not like the first. This is what happened, but the second portrait did not turn out any more flattering than the first. Pellerin ended up buying them both, to prevent them from being seen in public.

Some people have pointed to the influence of Cubism in the works from 1913 to 1917. Matisse himself later confessed that the success of Cubism caused him a great deal of anguish, as he felt he was almost alone "in not joining the direction that was acquiring more and more followers." In this period, however, he found that "methods of modern construction," which necessarily reflected Cubism, gave him the best means of self-expression in a fragmented, anxious time.

Looking back at early-twentieth-century art, many art historians have pointed to Matisse and Picasso as the two giants of the time. Because the two men had very different personalities as well as artistic styles, it was easy to contrast them and reduce their differences to formulas: Picasso's art is conceptual,

White and Pink Head. 1914–15
As in *The Moroccans* and *Portrait of Auguste Pellerin (II),* Matisse here used black as a major component of the painting. While the Impressionists before him avoided using black, Matisse considered it an important and indispensable color.

Portrait of Greta Prozor. 1916
Greta Prozor was an actress married to one of Matisse's pupils. Before Matisse began working on the portrait, he asked her about the theater to get her talking. When she became animated, he suddenly interrupted her and quickly sketched several remarkable drawings. Then he turned to the canvas, but, dissatisfied with the colors, he stopped. Later, without the model in front of him, he finished it, drawing on his imagination for the colors.

Matisse's decorative; Picasso's about form, Matisse's about color; Picasso's about dissonance and fragmentation, Matisse's about harmony and unity.

While some of these oppositions contain germs of truth, the reality was much more complex. Matisse described their relationship to Verdet: "Our differences were amicable. Sometimes, strangely, our points of view met. Picasso and I were in one another's confidence. We mutually gave one another a great deal in those exchanges. We cared passionately about our respective technical problems. There is no question that we each benefited from the other."

The two artists met in 1906 and exchanged paintings in 1907. They visited each other in their studios and gave each other gifts. Picasso's companion Françoise Gilot later wrote, "Toward Picasso, Matisse acted almost like a father, which made it easier for them to get along. In their conversations, Picasso took the active role, Matisse the passive. Like a dancer, Picasso tried to charm Matisse, but it was always Matisse who won over Pablo."

Was it possible for these two artists to avoid clashes or a feeling of rivalry? The many differences between them prevented this from happening, as well as those things – the most important from the human point of view – that united them. When Picasso learned that Matisse had undertaken a project for a chapel, he was upset, being a Communist and an atheist. Some months later, Matisse had the opportunity to touch this sensitive spot. He recalled that he told Picasso, "'Yes, I pray when all goes badly. So do you, and you know it very well. We throw ourselves into prayer to rediscover the climate of our first communion. And you do it as well.' He did not say no."

They formed a pair unprecedented in the history of world art, which they both understood. Matisse once told Picasso, "We must talk to each other as much as we can. When one of us dies, there will be some things the other will never be able to talk of with anyone else." And after Matisse died, Picasso said, "Now I have to work for the both of us." And, in fact, the very bright, pure colors he used at that time would have pleased Matisse.

Portrait of Auguste Pellerin (II). 1917
Matisse agreed to paint businessman Auguste Pellerin, who possessed the greatest collection of Cézanne's paintings in France. Even so, the artist did not flatter his sitter; stripping the subject down to his essentials, Matisse portrayed a dried-up, severe old man.

Matisse in Nice

When Matisse went to introduce himself to Auguste Renoir, "crippled and shrunken in his armchair, his eyes sharp and piercing under his gray cap," the younger artist was a painter with an international reputation, highly acclaimed and loudly denounced all over the world. His art had been exhibited in New York and Moscow, Berlin and London and had been discussed in a great many languages. For his part, "Renoir was evidently astonished," recalled a contemporary, art critic Georges Besson, "by the apparition of such an impeccable, sumptuous person, whose pale felt hat harmonized with his ample Shetland wool overcoat of a rare color – chosen by a painter's eye."

Matisse had gone south in 1917 in search of the sun to help cure his bronchitis. When he arrived in Nice, it was raining. For several weeks, he painted interiors, mostly of his hotel room, while he waited for the rain to stop. Just as he was beginning to give up, the sun emerged. Matisse fell in love with the silvery light and the splendid tropical plants and trees that grew in the area, which reminded him of Morocco, and adopted Nice as his home base.

He quickly fell into a routine that included, besides the long sessions of painting and drawing, practicing the violin (in a bathroom so as not to disturb his neighbors), and visiting and receiving friends. He moved several times, from one hotel to another, then to a villa. At one time, writer and art historian Raymond Escholier observed over three hundred birds that Matisse kept in a single room – blackbirds, pigeons, parakeets, rare species. In his seclusion, animals reminded him how endlessly diverse nature was, and how insistent its life. Much as he loved animals, however, he rarely put them in his paintings. A cat once accompanied a portrait of his daughter, but it was placed there to set off the young girl's softness, not as a character in itself. In his work, Matisse was drawn to human

Detail of *The Blue Eyes*. 1935

qualities above all. As he wrote in his "Notes of a Painter," "What interests me most is neither still life nor landscape, but the human figure."

Demoralized by the war and weary after a decade spent pushing the boundaries of painting, Matisse felt "I had to catch my breath, to relax and forget my worries, far from Paris," as he later told André Verdet. He turned to an art that was gentler, using delicate color harmonies suitable to the special serene light of Nice. Small landscapes painted on the hills above Nice, views of the sea from his windows, tender interiors, bouquets of flowers – all are bathed in the enchanting and soothing light of the south of France.

Above: Matisse visited Les Collettes, Renoir's house at Cagnes-sur-Mer. in 1918
Left to right: Claude Renoir, Greta Prozor, Matisse, Pierre Renoir, and Auguste Renoir.

Decorative Figure on an Ornamental Ground. 1925
A turning point in Matisse's art, this picture displays Matisse's reaction against the immediate popularity of his Odalisques. He made the female figure into a strong presence of verticals and horizontals to hold its own against the luxuriant background of curvilinear arabesques.

Matisse also began a long series of paintings of women, nude or embellished with scarves, mantillas, Oriental costumes, hats. This group came to be known as the Odalisques. Matisse explained, "The Odalisques were the bounty of a happy nostalgia, a lovely, vivid dream, and the almost ecstatic, enchanted days and nights of the Moroccan climate. I felt an irresistible need to express that ecstasy, that divine unconcern, in corresponding colored rhythms, rhythms of sunny and lavish figures and colors."

A group of refined paintings and drawings featured an eighteen-year-old model named Antoinette wearing a fluffy hat – made by Matisse himself – inspired by Alexandre Dumas's *The Three Musketeers*. In one of these, *The White Plumes*, Matisse placed her against a red background so that the young woman, whose yellow dress matches the color of the crown of the hat, resembles a statue of ivory. A more exotic painting, *Odalisque with Red Culottes*, shows a reclining partly nude woman. Her body is presented as if it were a jewel set off by the colorful Near Eastern tiles and textiles that surround her.

Many of Matisse's admirers were taken aback by the change of style. Compared with his earlier innovative works, these pictures struck them as "easy" and "charming." They accused

The Plumed Hat. 1919

White Plumes. 1919
For a period after the war, European art returned to classic principles and motifs. The series by Matisse of a young girl wearing a wide-brimmed hat recalls comparable images by Rubens, Van Dyck, and Rembrandt.

Odalisque with Red Culottes. 1921
Henriette Darricarrère, a favorite model of Matisse, posed for this painting, the first bought by the government of France for the Luxembourg Museum, which held the state's collection of modern art. The artist had been an important and internationally recognized force in French culture for some time, so this was a rather late gesture of official recognition for Matisse.

Matisse of having reached the end of his development. Others understood that Matisse was only mining his talents in a different vein. One of the critics called Matisse's odalisques obedient instruments on which he was playing his refined song.

In works like *Decorative Figure on an Ornamental Ground*, Matisse finally combined the softness and decorativeness of the Odalisques with the kind of strong construction that made his earlier compositions so powerful. Against such a complicated, highly patterned ground, Matisse had to simplify and strengthen the lines of the figure.

Nude with Blue Cushion Beside a Fireplace. 1925

By 1930, Matisse decided he needed a change of scene, a different space and light, to generate new ideas. He set off on a voyage to Tahiti that took him through the United States. With its "immense, immense" spaces and "dazzling light," America bowled him over. He found the light of New York—"very pure, ethereal, a crystalline light"—almost as impressive as that of the Pacific. From Tahiti he wrote to the painter Pierre Bonnard, "[I] lived twenty days on a 'coral isle': pure light, pure air, pure color: diamond sapphire emerald turquoise. Wonderful fish. Accomplished absolutely nothing except bad photos."

Less than two months after he returned to Paris, Matisse went back to the United States for the second time.

While he was there, he received a commission from a collector, Dr. Albert Barnes, to execute a large decorative mural. This brought him back to the United States for his third trip in the same year, to study the space where the mural was to go.

During the next two years, Matisse concentrated his efforts on this mural. He chose to make a new composition based on the subject of *Dance*, the painting he had created for Sergei Shchukin over twenty years before. As the new *Dance* was to be much bigger – almost fifty feet long and over twelve feet high – it called for a different approach. The earlier work, which Matisse had made without seeing the space for which it was intended, was fundamentally an enlarged easel painting. From the beginning, Matisse conceived of the Barnes mural as an architectural decoration made for a specific site. In order to achieve the right proportions, Matisse painted big pieces of paper with colors and then cut them into shapes. He pinned these to the walls of a large studio he rented just for this project and designed his composition by moving these pieces around. Once he was ready to paint, he fixed a charcoal crayon to the end of a six-foot-long bamboo stick to draw the enormous figures. When he began to paint, he found that the areas of color demanded adjustments in the design. After discarding a completed version of the mural and entirely repainting it, he escorted it across the Atlantic and saw it installed.

While Matisse was working on the mural, he found it hard to paint on the easel. But this man, described by Japanese artist Riichiro Kawashima as one who "always keeps a pencil in his hand, even while talking to people or smoking a cigarette," needed another outlet. He found it in the project of creating a series of etchings for a book of poems by Stéphane Mallarmé. These were not literal illustrations but equivalent works of art: "an ensemble in concert," as Matisse described it. He viewed the page and the type as elements of his design. As he saw it, "The problem was to balance the two pages – one white, with the etching, the other comparatively black, with the type. . . . I can compare my two pages to two objects taken up by a juggler. His white ball and black ball are like my two pages, the light one and the dark one; so different, yet face to face. In spite of the differences between two objects, the art of the juggler makes a harmonious whole in the eyes of the spectator."

Matisse considered his line drawing the purest and most direct translation of his emotions. He etched in a very even, thin line, omitting all minor details, leaving a powerful sensation of form that matched the mythological subject of *Dance*.

Matisse at work on the first version of *Dance* for the Barnes Foundation, near Philadelphia. 1931

At the same time, Matisse turned to sculpture. With very different means, he created another powerful sensation of form, especially in *The Back (IV)*, the last and most abstract of a series of sculptures of a woman's back, begun in 1909. Matisse made sculptures through most of his career. However, he told art critic Georges Charbonnier, "I myself have done sculpture as the complement of my studies. I did sculpture when I was tired of painting. For a change of medium. But I sculpted as a painter. I did not sculpt like a sculptor. Sculpture does not say what painting says."

Even so, Matisse seems to have had a clear idea of what sculpture says, as shown in his own work and in the advice he gave to his students, recorded by Sarah Stein: "In addition to the sensations one derives from a drawing, a sculpture must invite us to handle it as an object; just so the sculptor must feel, in making it, the particular demands for volume and mass."

When Matisse finally returned to painting in the mid-1930s, he also returned to the subject of beautiful women, this time without Oriental costumes and settings. Matisse claimed, "My models, human figures, are . . . the principal theme in my work. I depend entirely on my model, whom I observe at liberty, and then I decide on the pose which best suits *her nature*."

Dance. 1932–33

After Matisse painted the two large panels representing dance in 1909–10, one of them for Shchukin, he returned to the motif several times, and it became a kind of trademark. After the panel for Shchukin, his most important version of the theme is this giant mural made for American collector Dr. Albert Barnes. Convinced that every space and scale called for different qualities of line, color, and composition, Matisse refused simply to blow up a smaller work to fit the larger space and instead worked on the exact size of the walls intended for the mural.

The four relief sculptures, called *The Back, I, II, III,* and *IV,* were made over the course of some twenty years, but all relate closely.

Matisse sketching in the park called Bois de Boulogne in Paris.

The Swan. An illustration for the book, *Poésies de Stéphane Mallarmé.* 1932

Woman in Blue. 1937

Curiously, no art historian has ever compared this painting with sixteenth- and seventeenth-century portraits of aristocrats and royalty. Matisse achieved the effect of grandeur with simple, pure colors and lines.

One of Matisse's constant models from 1934 on, a young Russian named Lydia Delectorskaya, was initially employed to help run the household. Then she became progressively Matisse's studio assistant, secretary, and "devoted collaborator," according to the artist. With her natural, unselfconscious manner and vivid spirit, she served as an ideal model. *The Blue Eyes* shows her sunk in reverie, her large blue eyes fixed on a world invisible to the spectator but clearly indicating an intense inner life.

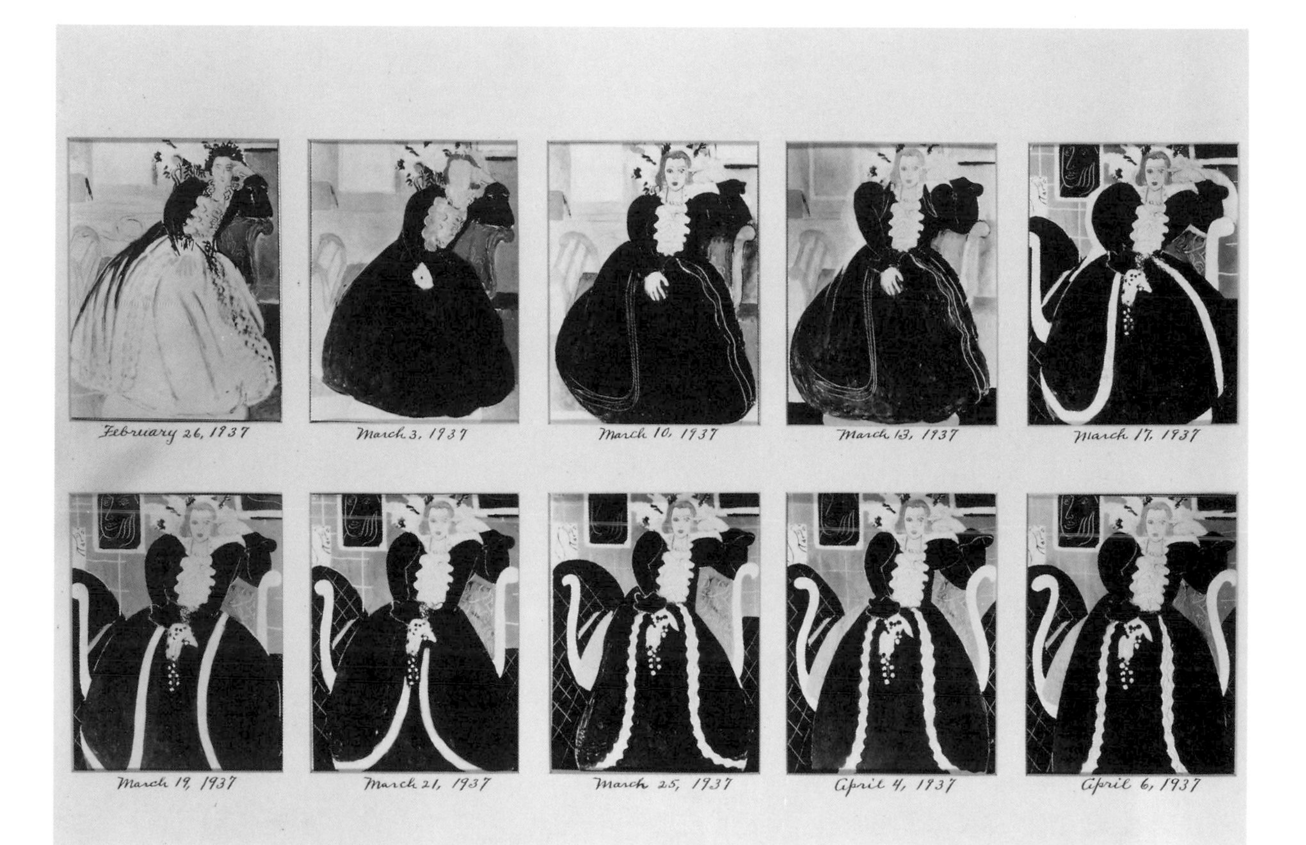

Progressive studies of *Woman in Blue*. 1937

The effect of simplicity in Matisse's works usually resulted from hard work that cannot be detailed. Here, however, these photographs of *Woman in Blue* at different stages reveal the creative process: from a more realistic approach to one that was increasingly abstract and decorative.

The Blue Eyes. 1935
This romantic image is one of the most glorious tributes to the physical and spiritual beauty of woman in modern art.

In *Woman in Blue*, also called *The Large Blue Robe and Mimosas*, Lydia posed in an opulent theatrical dress that she sewed herself. Matisse repainted this picture ten times, at first representing the model and her dress realistically and then simplifying it until the lines merge into a single, harmonious arabesque; that is, a flowing linear decorative design. While the blue predominates, it stands out because of the use of the two other primary colors. The yellow of the mimosa glows behind the model's head like a kind of aureole.

Drawing in Color

In the late 1930s Matisse continued working on a series of bright, decorative paintings featuring models in exotic costumes, Romanian blouses, or Persian robes, surrounded by plants, flowers, and fruit. He branched out into the decorative arts – designs for a tapestry, a glass vase, an overmantel – and scenery and costumes for the ballet.

Meanwhile, the ominous events taking place in Nazi Germany touched even Matisse in his peaceful garden in Nice. The Nazis, having decided that all forms of modern art were dangerous for the spiritual health of their country, removed Matisse's works from German museums, along with the art of such outstanding modern artists as Gauguin, Van Gogh, Picasso, Chagall, Kandinsky, and others. They put these paintings together and held an exhibition called "Degenerate Art" – ironically, the most widely attended cultural event on the continent. Some of Matisse's paintings were put up for sale at an auction. Many important art dealers were Jewish, and they decided to boycott the auction in protest. The boycott was successful, as many works went unsold – so the Nazi authorities spitefully destroyed a lot of pictures. One painting that fortunately escaped this fate was *Bathers with a Turtle,* which Matisse's son Pierre, an art dealer in New York, purchased for a young American collector, Joseph Pulitzer (who, as he was Jewish, did not want to participate directly in the auction).

Two months later, German troops invaded Poland, setting off World War II. Less than a year later, France fell to the German armies. Pierre Matisse urged his father to flee, and Matisse, who had been invited to teach in the United States, in San Francisco, made ready to leave. When he reached the Spanish border "the inexhaustible stream of refugees" he saw there made him change his mind. He explained to Pierre in a letter, "When I saw everything in such a mess I had them

Detail of *Circus,* from *Jazz.* 1943

reimburse my ticket. I realized that I should have felt like a deserter. If everyone who is worth anything runs away, what will remain of our country?"

He returned to Nice. His wife, from whom he had separated just a year before, lived in Paris with their daughter Marguerite. Both were active in the Resistance, which led to their arrest and imprisonment in 1944.

In 1941, Matisse had a very close brush with death. Suffering from chronic intestinal discomfort, he went to Lyons for what he thought would be a simple operation with no real danger. His problem turned out to be cancer, and, as he wrote to Bonnard, "My operation was a tremendous upset – they say here that I came out of it somewhat miraculously." His recovery was equally perilous. Some traveling blood clots forced him "to lie perfectly still and wait" for three months. It was almost five months before he was able to get back to Nice.

Compelled to remain in bed for much of the day, Matisse busied himself with drawing. Wielding a piece of charcoal, he set down a "theme," then made numerous "variations" in pencil or pen. In all, he created seventeen groups of drawings. He also worked on more books of illustrations. Taking refuge from the war and his physical distress in the love lyrics of the sixteenth-century poet Pierre de Ronsard,

Head of a Woman. 1937

Right: *Icarus*. 1943

Circus. Plate II from *Jazz.* 1947

This gouache cutout of a pennant, red carpet, and trapeze artist is dated 1946 but was created in 1943, when Matisse wanted to call his book *Circus,* and he saw this as the cover. In 1946 he decided to add text to the book, and the following year it was published, using prints made with the linoleum-cut technique.

he selected several of the poems and made over one hundred lithographs of leaves, flowers, fruit, young girls' faces, and nightingales. Lydia Delectorskaya recalled that he "was very proud of their throats swelling in song." He found a different kind of comfort in the poetry of Charles d'Orléans, the duke who started to write while a prisoner of the English from 1415 to 1440. For this project, Matisse wrote the poems out by hand and decorated the pages using colored pencils.

He hand-wrote the text – this time of his own composition – for another book project called *Jazz*. He made illustrations, "in vivid and violent tones," by cutting out shapes from painted papers, a medium he first employed for the Barnes mural *Dance*. These images, Matisse said in the corresponding text, emerged from his "memories of the circus, popular tales, or travel." He almost titled the book *Circus* but decided that the cutouts, with their free forms and bold colors, corresponded perfectly to the improvisational spirit of jazz.

Matisse called his collage method "drawing with scissors." He found it greatly liberating since, as he later explained, "Cut-out paper allows me to draw in color. For me it is a matter of simplification. Instead of drawing the contour and then filling in with color – one modifying the other – I draw directly in color. . . . That simplification guarantees precision in the union of the two modes of expression, which are then one." Only a few years earlier, Matisse, professing himself "totally discouraged," had lamented to Bonnard, "My drawing and my painting are separating." Cutouts gave him a way to put them back together.

Matisse went on to create several large-scale cutouts. Two of the most abstract are *The Snail* and *Memory of Oceania*. The snail he evoked simply by the movement of the colored squares in a slow spiral. The second work is an evocation of Tahiti and its colors: "diamond sapphire emerald turquoise."

The technique of cutouts helped Matisse to realize his last great project, creating decorations for the Dominican Chapel of the Rosary in Vence, a small town near Nice. In 1942, he had hired as his nurse a young refugee named Monique Bourgeois. She not only changed his bandages, she also read to him at night when he could not sleep. He became attached to her and paid for her medical studies. By the end of the war, both were living in Vence. Matisse had moved there to avoid the danger of bombardment, while Monique had come to be treated for tuberculosis at a nursing home run by Dominican nuns. She ended up becoming a nun, Sister Jacques, and helped cure sick young women at the home.

On a visit to Matisse in the autumn of 1947 she told him that the community was going to enlarge or rebuild their small chapel. Since he knew that Sister

Jacques loved to draw, he convinced her to make a design for the stained-glass window of the chapel. He showed the design to Brother Rayssiguier, a young Dominican with some architectural training, who grinned at the naive drawing and convinced Matisse to undertake the design himself. Four years later, Matisse wrote to the archbishop of Nice to humbly present his work on the Chapel of the Rosary, work that had consumed his being. He designed all the decorations, from the stained-glass windows and ceramic murals to the bronze Crucifixion, and worked out all the details, from the carpeting, tile roof, and wrought-iron crosses to the robes worn by the priests. It turned out to be his most complete joining of art to architecture.

While Matisse himself was not religious, his feeling for art and its ancient traditions and a deep respect for almost two thousand years of his ancestors' faith combined to create a special atmosphere. "I want those who enter my chapel," said Matisse, "to feel purified and delivered from their burdens." He told Sister Jacques, "We shall have a chapel where all can experience hope. Whatever sins a person carries with him, he can leave them at the door, the way the Muslims leave the dust of the roads together with their sandals at the door of the mosque."

Françoise Gilot described Matisse's

The Chapel of the Rosary at Vence.

Matisse modeling a crucifix for the Chapel of the Rosary at Vence. 1949

working process. The eighty-year-old artist "had paper fixed to the ceiling over his bed, and at night, since he didn't sleep much, he would draw on it with a piece of charcoal attached to the end of a long bamboo stick, sketching out the portrait of St. Dominic and other elements of the decoration. Later, he would roll around in his wheelchair and transfer his drawings to large ceramic squares covered with a semi-matte enamel on which he could draw in black."

In the chapel, the black-and-white ceramic panels faced a wall of stained-glass windows with a design of leaves in blue, green, and yellow, representing the Tree of Life. Matisse composed the windows using colored cutouts. He conceived of the tile panels as the "spiritual essence" of the interior that "explain the meaning of the monument." To the panels of Saint Dominic and of the Virgin and Child he gave a "serenity [that] has a character of tranquil contemplation." The third panel, the Stations of the Cross, "marks the encounter of the artist with the great tragedy of Christ" and is "tempestuous."

Matisse was exceedingly proud of what he called "his chapel," considering it

A priest at the Chapel of the Rosary at Vence wearing a chasuble designed by Matisse. 1952

his crowning achievement. He told Georges Charbonnier he wanted visitors to the chapel, believers or not, "to experience a lightening of the spirit." He wanted it to be a place "where thought is clarified, where feeling itself is lightened." In 1952, he told André Verdet, "If people knew what Matisse, supposedly the painter of happiness, had gone through, the anguish and tragedy he had to overcome to manage to capture that light which has never left him, if people knew all that, they would also realize that this happiness, this light, this dispassionate wisdom which seems to be mine, are sometimes well-deserved, given the severity of my trials."

After finishing the chapel, Matisse made several magnificent cutouts. He had found in them his "ultimate method." Not long before he died, on November 3, 1954, he used cutouts to design a rose window for a church on Nelson Rockefeller's Pocantico Hills estate. The simple, beautiful color radiating a glowing light, the composition's feeling of balance and serenity" – qualities that Matisse achieved at cost – create a fitting memorial to the artist who dreamed of "an art of balance, purity, and serenity" and dedicated his entire life to achieving it.

List of Illustrations

The Museum of Modern Art, New York. Mrs. Simon Guggenheim Fund. Photograph © 1995 The Museum of Modern Art, New York

Page 48: *Goldfish.* 1912. Oil on canvas, 51¼ x 38⅛". The State Pushkin Museum of Fine Arts, Moscow

Page 50 (left): *Landscape Viewed from a Window.* 1912. Oil on canvas, 45¼ x 31½". The State Pushkin Museum of Fine Arts, Moscow

Page 50 (right): *On the Terrace.* 1912. Oil on canvas, 45⅝ x 39⅜". The State Pushkin Museum of Fine Arts, Moscow

Page 51: *The Casbah Gate.* 1912. Oil on canvas, 45½ x 31½". The State Pushkin Museum of Fine Arts, Moscow

Page 52: *Moroccan Café.* 1912–13. Tempera on canvas, 69¼" x 6'10¾". The State Hermitage Museum, St. Petersburg

Pages 54–55: *The Moroccans.* 1915–16. Oil on canvas, 71⅜" x 9'2". The Museum of Modern Art, New York. Gift of Mr. and Mrs. Samuel A. Marx. Photograph: © 1995 The Museum of Modern Art

Page 57: *White and Pink Head.* 1914–15. Oil on canvas, 29½ x 18½". Musée National d'Art Moderne, Centre Georges Pompidou, Paris

Page 58: *Portrait of Greta Prozor.* 1916. Oil on canvas, 57½ x 37¾". Musée National d'Art Moderne, Centre Georges Pompidou, Paris

Page 61: *Portrait of Auguste Pellerin (II).* 1917. Oil on canvas, 59 x 37⅞". Musée National d'Art Moderne, Centre Georges Pompidou, Paris

Page 62: Detail of *The Blue Eyes*

Page 64: *Decorative Figure on an Ornamental Ground.* 1925. Oil on canvas, 51⅛ x 38½". Musée National d'Art Moderne, Centre Georges Pompidou, Paris. Photograph: Georges Routhier

Page 65: Renoir's house, Les Collettes. Photograph: Halvorsen Archives, Oslo

Page 66: *The Plumed Hat.* 1919. Graphite pencil on paper, 20⅞ x 14⅜". Detroit Institute of Arts, Founders Society. Bequest of John S. Newberry

Page 67: *White Plumes.* 1919. Oil on canvas, 28¾ x 23¾". The Minneapolis Institute of Arts, The William Hood Dunwoody Fund

Page 68: *Odalisque with Red Culottes.* 1921. Oil on canvas, 26⅜ x 33⅛". Musée National d'Art Moderne, Centre Georges Pompidou, Paris

Page 69: *Nude with Blue Cushion Beside a Fireplace.* 1925. Lithograph, 25 x 18⅞". The Museum of Modern Art, New York. Gift of Abby Aldrich Rockefeller (by exchange). Photograph: Geoffrey Clements, New York

Page 71: Matisse at work. Photograph: Barnes Foundation Archives

Pages 72–73: *The Dance II.* 1932–33. Oil on canvas, 12'7½" x 15'7" (left); 13'1½" x 16'5" (center); 12'3½" x 15'5" (right). The Barnes Foundation, Merion, Pennsylvania. Photographs © 1995 The Barnes Foundation

Page 74: *The Swan.* Etching from the book, *Poesies de Stéphane Mallarmé.* Lausanne: Albert Skira & Cie, 1932. One of 29 etchings, each page 13⅛ x 9⅞". Baltimore Museum of Art

Page 75 (above): *Back I, II, III, IV.* 1930. Bronze reliefs, each 6'2½" x 45" x 7". Hirshhorn Museum and Sculpture Garden, Smithsonian Institution, Washington, D.C.

Page 75 (below): Matisse sketching

Page 76: *Woman in Blue.* 1937. Oil on canvas, 36½ x 29". Philadelphia Museum of Art. Gift of Mrs. John Wintersteen

Page 77: Progressive studies of *Woman in Blue*, 1937. Formerly collection Mrs. John Wintersteen

Page 78: *The Blue Eyes.* 1935. Oil on canvas, 15 x 18". The Baltimore Museum of Art, The Cone Collection, formed by Dr. Claribel Cone and Miss Etta Cone of Baltimore, Maryland

Page 80: Detail of *Circus*

Page 82: *Head of a Woman.* 1937. Pen and ink on paper, 24⅙ x 16 3/16". The Santa Barbara Museum of Art. Gift of Wright S. Ludington

Page 83: *Icarus.* 1943. Cut and pasted paper, gouache, 16⅝ x 10⅝". Ecole des Beaux-Arts, Paris

Page 84: *Circus.* Plate II from *Jazz.* Paris: E. Teriade, 1947. Pochoir, printed in color, composition: 16⅝ x 25⅝". The Museum of Modern Art, New York. The Louis E. Stern Collection. Photograph © 1995 The Museum of Modern Art

Page 86: The Chapel of the Rosary, Vence. Photograph: Barry

Page 87: Matisse at work. Photograph: Helene Adant, Paris

Page 88: The Chapel of the Rosary, Vence. Photograph: Helene Adant, Paris

Page 89: The Chapel of the Rosary, Vence. Photograph: Helene Adant, Paris

Index

Italic page numbers refer to captions and illustrations.